SACRED SIGNS

by

ROMANO GUARDINI

Translated by Grace Branham

Drawings by Wm. V. Cladek

PIO DECIMO PRESS

St. Louis 15, Mo.

IMPRIMATUR

✠ JOSEPH E. RITTER

Archbishop of St. Louis

November 14, 1955

CONTENTS

Page

Translator's Preface 3

Introduction 9

The Sign of the Cross 13

The Hands 15

Kneeling 19

Standing 21

Walking 25

Striking the Breast 29

Steps 33

Doors 37

Candles 41

Holy Water 45

Fire 49

Ashes 53

Incense 57

Light and Heat 61

Bread and Wine 65

Linen 69

The Altar 73

The Chalice 77

The Paten 79

Blessing 81

Space Sanctified 85

Bells 89

Time Sanctified 93

The Name of God 101

TRANSLATOR'S PREFACE

THAT this unpretentious little book, written so long ago as the first world war, should still be thought worth retranslating and republishing is a tribute to its value as an introduction to the liturgical life. But that so elementary an introduction should be as much needed now as then, at least in America, is a tribute also to the slow advance of the liturgical movement, if that is to be the name given to the new life now quickening in the church. Never movement moved so slowly to remain a movement. Over forty years ago St. Pius X reopened the world of the liturgy, and with all his authority as Pope and man of God urged clergy and people to enter into their inheritance. The Pope has been canonized, but has he been obeyed?

In some places, magnificently. One may say that he has been obeyed wherever the liturgy was well understood. It was from the great Benedictine Monasteries, Solesmes, Beuron, Maria Laach, that the influence spread which has worked such wonders in France, Germany and Austria. We in America hardly yet know what the Pope desired. A priest, pressed by a friend, answered that it was hard enough on the people to have to worship in an unfamiliar language without forcing on them in addition an unfamiliar music. But the people, given a little encouragement, will sing the church music with all their heart. Last Easter the Baltimore Cathedral was filled with the massive voice of the congregation pouring out Creed and Gloria, and responding to the single voice of the priest; and while the mass went silently forward at the altar, the music of the seminary choir, freed from the double load of choir and congregation, reached the worshipping heart in all its intricate beauty. In this fulfilment of the Pope's so long deferred hope the joy and satisfaction (and relief) of clergy and people alike proved how right he was.

But the new life, with its source and centre in the liturgy, goes out from there in every direction. It springs up in the work of an artist like Roualt, in the pastoral work of men like Parsch, and of those French priests who are carrying the word to every soul in their geographical parishes, or laboring side by side with the workers in factory and mine, in the strong impact on Protestantism of Guardini and Karl Adam, in the confident Biblical scholarship of the French Dominicans. All are parts, as a reviewer in the *Literary Supplement* of the *London Times* put it, of "a coherent system that has gone back to the fountain head." The book under review called it a Catholic Renaissance, and the reviewer added that it was a second Reformation, which may have "among its effects the healing of the breaches caused by the earlier and less radical one of four centuries ago."

If, so far as we in America have failed to catch fire, our failure is owing rather to inability than to a defect of will. Behind the liturgy is the Bible; and Catholic education here, whatever its merits, has not been such as to make the Bible a congenial book. It is a slander to say that Catholics are not allowed to read the Bible; it is no slander to say that by and large they do not read it. Our religious education addresses itself to the intellect and the will, — our "spiritual faculties." It has resulted (no mean achievement) in moral firmness and mental precision. But the formulas of the Catechism do not enable us to read the two great works provided by God for our education, — created nature and the Written Word. In these are addressed not only our intelligences and our wills, but the entire human creature, body and soul, with his imagination, passions, appetites, secular experiences, the whole complex in which intellect and will are inextricably mingled. Cultivated apart, and as it were out of context, our noblest faculties may grow dry and superficial. Man being of a piece, if his appetite for beauty, joy, freedom, love, is left unnourished, his so called spiritual nature contracts and hardens.

The Bible is literature, not science, and as literature it engages man's full nature. And external nature, as the Bible presupposes it, is not a system of forces intended primarily (if at all) for man's scientific and economic mastery. The Bible takes the ancient poetic view which rests upon direct insight. Nature is a "macrocosm," and it is epitomized in man, the "microcosm." Nature is human nature written large.

It is a miraculous appearance drawn from a primordial chaos back into which it would sink were it not sustained in fleeting being by the substantial hand of God. Man and nature are inseparable parts of one creation, and our being, like our justice, is God's momentary gift.

Guardini's *Sacred Signs* was designed to begin our reeducation. It assumes that correspondence between man and nature, matter and meaning, which is the basis of the Sacramental System and made possible the Incarnation. Man, body and soul together, is made in the image and likeness of God. His hand, like God's, is an instrument of power. In the Bible "hand" means power. Man's feet stand for something also he shares with God, as does his every limb, feature and organ. The writers of the Bible had an inward awareness of what the body means. As the head and the heart denote wisdom and love, so do the 'bones,' 'reins,' and 'flesh' signify some aspect of God written into our human body. The contemplation of the body of Christ should teach us what this deeper meaning is.

The next step in our reeducation after the symbolism of the body, which once pointed out we instinctively perceive, is for modern man something of a leap. He will have to abandon or leave to one side the notions instilled into him by modern science. Symbolically, if not physically, nature is composed of only four elements: earth, air, water and fire. Earth, humble, helpless earth, stands for man, and water, air, and fire for the gifts from the sky that make him live and fructify. Combined in sun, moon, and stars, they represent Christ, the Church and the Saints, though perhaps rather by allegory than symbolism. The sea signifies untamed and lawless nature, the primordial chaos; the mountains signify the faithfulness of God.

Objects, things, are not the only symbols. Their use and function, again stretching the term, is a sort of immaterial symbol. The positions and movements of human hands and feet may symbolize God's action. Direction, dimension, are also symbolic, and so are those two philosophical puzzles, time and space, which provide the conditions of human action and progress. The course of the sun is a sign to us of time; by prayer we eternalize time; and the church breaks up the sun's daily course into three or seven canonical hours of prayer. Its yearly course, which governs the seasons and their agricultural operations, signifies to us, as it has to religious man from the beginning, life, death and resurrection, and in revealed history God has accommodated the great works of our redemption to the appropriate seasons.

The last field of symbolism the sacred signs indicate to us is one that causes us no surprise. Art from the beginning has been symbolic. The Temple of Solomon like the "heathen" temples was built to symbolize the earth, and Christian Churches are (or were) built upon the model of the Temple in Jerusalem and of its exemplar the Temple in Heaven from which the earth was modeled. The axis of a Christian Church, its geometric shape and numerical proportions, the objects used in its worship, the disposition of its windows, its ornamentation to the last petal or arc, all carry our minds to the divine meaning behind the visible form.

For the modern American Catholic, as for the modern American non-Catholic, these vast symbolic regions of nature, man and art are lapsed worlds, unknown, unbelieved-in. *Sacred Signs* furnishes us with a clue. If we pick it up and follow it we shall come, as it were naturally, to reexercise over them and in them the kingship and priesthood conferred on us by God, which also, largely, has lapsed. We shall carry, as the saying is, our religion into our daily lives, and build our houses, like our churches, about a central hearth of God's charity, remember in our entrances the double nature of him who called himself the door, and in our windows who is signified by light. Every act of daily living would again take on meaning, temporal and eternal, and we should again become the doer, which man naturally is, instead of the passive receptionist he threatens to become.

INTRODUCTION

THIS little book has been in circulation some ten years. It was written to help open up the world of the liturgy. That world will never be made accessible by accounts of how the certain rites and prayers came into existence and under what influences, or by explanations of the ideas underlying liturgical practices. Those ideas may be true and profound, but they are not apparent in the present liturgy, and can be deduced from it only by scholarly research. The liturgy is not a matter of ideas, but of actual things, and of actual things as they now are, not as they were in the past. It is a continuous movement carried on by and through us, and its forms and actions issue from our human nature. To show how it arose and developed brings us no nearer to it, and no more does this or that learned interpretation. What does help is to discern in the living liturgy what underlies the visible sign, to discover the soul from the body, the hidden and spiritual from the external and material. The liturgy has taken its outward shape from a divine and hidden series of happenings. It is sacramental in its nature.

So the procedure that avails is to study those actions that are still in present day use, those visible signs which believers have received and made their own and use to express the "invisible grace." For this it is not liturgical scholarship that is needed, — though the two things are not separable, — but liturgical education. We need to be shown how, or by some means incited, to see and feel and make the sacred signs ourselves.

It strikes me that the right and fruitful method is to start off in the simplest way with the elements out of which the higher liturgical forms have been constructed. Whatever in human nature responds to these elementary signs should be fanned into life. These signs are real symbols; consequently, by making them a fresh and vital experience of their own, people would get at the spirit which informs them, and arrive at the genuine symbol from the conventional sign. They might even again be caught up in the Christian process that sees and fashions the things of the spirit into visible forms, and do so freshly for themselves. After all, the person who makes the signs has been baptized, both soul and body, and therefore able to understand (this was the idea) the signs as sacred symbols and constituent parts of sacrament and sacramental. Then from the practice of them, which can be gained from these little sketches (which make no claim to completeness) he could move on to a deeper understanding of their meaning and justification.*

It is a real question whether something written under special circumstances, and growing out of the needs of a particular group, should be republished after so long an interval of time. There are other objections to these little essays of mine of which I am quite aware. They are not sufficiently objective; they meet no classified need. They are subjective, semi-poetic, casual and impressionistic, and all this apart from their obvious literary deficiencies. Yet it remains that basically they are right, and have a claim, consequently, in spite of sound objections, to republication. For if they do not attain the end for which they were written, at least they indicate it, and no other liturgical work comes readily to mind that does even that much any better.

One person who could do what they attempt both better and more appropriately, would be a mother who had herself been trained in the liturgy. She could teach her child the right way to make the sign of the cross, make him see what it is in himself the lighted candle stands for, show him in his little human person how to stand and carry himself in his Father's house, and never at any point with the least touch of aestheticism, simply as something the child sees, something he does, and not as an idea to hang gestures on.

Another competent person would be a teacher who shares the lives of his pupils. He could make them capable of experiencing and celebrating Sunday as the day it is, and feast days and the seasons of the church year. He could make them realize the meaning of doors or bells, or the interior arrangement of the church, or outdoor processions. These two, mother and teacher, could bring the sacred signs to life.

11

A short article by Maria Montessori, whose work in education is so significant, made me feel when I read it, that here was both the fulfillment of these ideas and their promise for the future. Her method is to teach by actual doing. In one of her schools the children take care of a vineyard and a wheatfield. They gather the grapes, sow and harvest the grain, and, as far as they can technically manage it, make, according to the rules of the church, wine and bread, and then carry them as their gifts to the altar. This kind of learning, together with the right kind of instruction, is liturgical education. For the approach to the liturgy is not by being told about it but by taking part in it.

To learn to see, to learn to do, these are the fundamental "skills" that make the groundwork for all the rest. The doing must of course be enlightened by lucid instruction and rooted in Catholic tradition, which they learn from their courses in history. And "doing" does not mean "practicing" in order to get a thing right. Doing is basic; it includes the whole human person with all his creative powers. It is the outcome in action of the child's own experience, of his own understanding, of his own ability to look and see.

When teachers such as these, out of their own experience, give instruction in the sacred signs, this little book may vanish into oblivion. Until then it has a claim, even an obligation, to say its say as well as it can.

MOOSHAUSEN in the *Swabian Alligau*

Spring, 1927

*See my book on Liturgical Education

12

THE SIGN OF THE CROSS

WHEN we cross ourselves, let it be with a real sign of
the cross. Instead of a small cramped gesture that gives
no notion of its meaning, let us make a large unhurried
sign, from forehead to breast, from shoulder to shoulder,
consciously feeling how it includes the whole of us, our
thoughts, our attitudes, our body and soul, every part of
us at once, how it consecrates and sanctifies us.

It does so because it is the sign of the universe and the sign of our redemption. On the cross Christ redeemed mankind. By the cross he sanctifies man to the last shred and fibre of his being. We make the sign of the cross before we pray to collect and compose ourselves and to fix our minds and hearts and wills upon God. We make it when we finish praying in order that we may hold fast the gift we have received from God. In temptations we sign ourselves to be strengthened; in dangers, to be protected. The cross is signed upon us in blessings in order that the fulness of God's life may flow into the soul and fructify and sanctify us wholly.

Think of these things when you make the sign of the cross. It is the holiest of all signs. Make a large cross, taking time, thinking what you do. Let it take in your whole being, — body, soul, mind, will, thoughts, feelings, your doing and not-doing, — and by signing it with the cross strengthen and consecrate the whole in the strength of Christ, in the name of the triune God.

THE HANDS

EVERY part of the body is an expressive instrument of
the soul. The soul does not inhabit the body as a man
inhabits a house. It lives and works in each member,
each fibre, and reveals itself in the body's every line,
contour and movement. But the soul's chief instruments
and clearest mirrors are the face and hands.

Of the face this is obviously true. But if you will
watch other people (or yourself), you will notice how

instantly every slightest feeling, — pleasure, surprise, suspense, — shows in the hand. A quick lifting of the hand or a flicker of the fingers say far more than words. By comparison with a language so natural and expressive the spoken word is clumsy. Next to the face, the part of the body fullest of mind is the hand. It is a hard strong tool for work, a ready weapon of attack and defence, — but also, with its delicate structure and network of innumerable nerves, it is adaptable, flexible, and highly sensitive. It is a skilful workmanlike contrivance for the soul to make herself known by. It is also an organ of receptivity for matter from outside ourselves. For when we clasp the extended hand of a stranger are we not receiving from a foreign source the confidence, pleasure, sympathy or sorrow that his hand conveys?

So it could not but be that in prayer, where the soul has so much to say to, so much to learn from, God, where she gives herself to him and receives him to herself, the hand should take on expressive forms.

When we enter into ourselves and the soul is alone with God, our hands closely interlock, finger clasped in finger, in a gesture of compression and control. It is as if we would prevent the inner current from escaping by conducting it from hand to hand and so back again to God who is within us, holding it there. It is as if we were collecting all our forces in order to keep guard over the hidden God, so that he who is mine and I who am his should be left alone together. Our hands take the same position when some dire need or pain weighs heavily on us and threatens to break out. Hand then locks in hand and the soul struggles with itself until it gets control and grows quiet again.

But when we stand in God's presence in heart-felt reverence and humility, the open hands are laid together palm against palm in sign of steadfast subjection and obedient homage, as if to say that the words we ourselves would speak are in good order, and that we are ready and attentive to hear the words of God. Or it may be a sign of inner surrender. These hands, our weapons of defence, are laid, as it were, tied and bound together between the hands of God.

In moments of jubilant thanksgiving when the soul is entirely open to God with every reserve done away with and every passage of its instrument unstopped, and it flows at the full outwards and upwards, then the hands are uplifted and spread apart with the palms up to let the river of the spirit stream out unhindered and to receive in turn the water for which it thirsts. So too when we long for God and cry out to him.

Finally when sacrifice is called for and we gather together all we are and all we have and offer ourselves to God with full consent, then we lay our arms over our breast and make with them the sign of the cross.

There is greatness and beauty in this language of the hands. The Church tells us that God has given us our hands in order that we may "carry our souls" in them. The Church is fully in earnest in the use she makes of the language of gesture. She speaks through it her inmost mind, and God gives ear to this mode of speaking.

Our hands may also indicate the goods we lack, — our unchecked impulses, our distractions, and other faults. Let us hold them as the Church directs and see to it that there is a real correspondence between the interior and exterior attitude.

In matters such as this we are on delicate ground. We would prefer not to talk about things of this order. Something within us objects. Let us then avoid all empty and unreal talk and concentrate the more carefully on the actual doing. That is a form of speech by which the plain realities of the body say to God what its soul means and intends.

KNEELING

WHEN a man feels proud of himself, he stands erect, draws himself to his full height, throws back his head and shoulders and says with every part of his body, I am bigger and more important than you. But when he is humble he feels his littleness, and lowers his head and shrinks into himself. He abases himself. And the greater the presence in which he stands the more deeply he abases himself; the smaller he becomes in his own eyes.

But when does our littleness so come home to us as when we stand in God's presence? He is the great God, who is today and yesterday, whose years are hundreds and thousands, who fills the place where we are, the city, the wide world, the measureless space of the starry sky, in whose eyes the universe is less than a particle of dust, all-holy, all-pure, all-righteous, infinitely high. He is so great, I so small, so small that beside him I seem hardly to exist, so wanting am I in worth and substance. One has no need to be told that God's presence is not the place in which to stand on one's dignity. To appear less presumptious, to be as little and low as we feel, we sink to our knees and thus sacrifice half our height; and to satisfy our hearts still further we bow down our heads, and our diminished stature speaks to God and says, Thou art the great God; I am nothing.

Therefore let not the bending of our knees be a hurried gesture, an empty form. Put meaning into it. To kneel, in the soul's intention, is to bow down before God in deepest reverence.

On entering a church, or in passing before the altar, kneel down all the way without haste or hurry, putting your heart into what you do, and let your whole attitude say, Thou art the great God. It is an act of humility, an act of truth, and everytime you kneel it will do your soul good.

STANDING

THE respect we owe to the infinite God requires of us a bearing suited to such a presence. The sense that we have of the greatness of His being, and, in His eyes, of the slightness of our own, is shown outwardly by our kneeling down to make ourselves small. But reverence has another way of expressing itself. When you are sitting down to rest or chat, and someone to whom you owe respect comes in and turns to speak to you, at once you stand up and remain standing so long as he is speaking and you are answering him. Why do we do this?

In the first place to stand up means that we are in possession of ourselves. Instead of sitting relaxed and at ease we take hold of ourselves; we stand, as it were, at attention, geared and ready for action. A man on his feet can come or go at once. He can take an order on the instant, or carry out an assignment the moment he is shown what is wanted.

Standing is the other side of reverence toward God. Kneeling is the side of worship in rest and quietness; standing is the side of vigilance and action. It is the respect of the servant in attendance, of the soldier on duty.

When the good news of the gospel is proclaimed, we stand up. Godparents stand when in the child's place they make the solemn profession of faith; children when they renew these promises at their first communion. Bridegroom and bride stand when they bind themselves at the altar to be faithful to their marriage vow. On these and the like occasions we stand up.

Even when we are praying alone, to pray standing may more forcibly express our inward state. The early Christians stood by preference. The "Orante," in the familiar catacomb representation, stands in her long flowing robes of a woman of rank and prays with outstretched hands, in perfect freedom, perfect obedience, quietly attending to the word, and in readiness to perform it with joy.

We may feel at times a sort of constraint in kneeling. One feels freer standing up, and in that case standing is the right position. But stand up straight: not leaning, both feet on the ground, the knees firm, not slackly bent, upright, in control. Prayer made thus is both free and obedient, both reverent and serviceable.

WALKING

WALKING, — how many people know how to walk? It is not hurrying along at a kind of run, or shuffling along at a snail's pace, but a composed and firm forward movement. There is spring in the tread of a good walker. He lifts, not drags, his heels. He is straight, not stoop-shouldered, and his steps are sure and even.

There is something uncommonly fine in the right kind of walking. It is a combination of freedom and discipline. It is poised, as if the walker were carrying a weight, yet proceeds with unhampered energy. In a man's walk there is a suggestion of bearing arms or burdens; in a woman's an attractive grace that reflects an inner world of peace.

And when the occasion is religious, what a beautiful thing walking can be! It is a genuine act of divine worship. Merely to walk into a church in reverent awareness that we are entering the house of the Most High, and in a special manner into his presence, may be "to walk before the Lord." Walking in a religious procession ought not to be what so often it is, pushing along out of step and staring about. To escort the Blessed Sacrament through the city streets, or through the fields, "his own possession," the men marching like soldiers, the married women in the dignity of motherhood, the young girls in the innocent charm of youth, the young men in their restrained strength, all praying in their hearts, should be a sight of festive gladness.

A penitential procession should be supplication in visible form. It should embody our guilt, and our desperate need of help, but also the Christian assurance that overrules them, — that as in man there is a power that is superior to all his other powers, the power of his untroubled will, so, above and beyond human guilt and distress there is the might of the living God.

Walking is the outward mark of man's essential and

peculiar nobility. It is the privilege of man alone to walk erect, his movement in his own power and choice. The upright carriage denotes the human being.

But we are more than human beings. We are, as the Bible calls us, the generation of God. We have been born of God into newness of life. Profoundly, through the Sacrament of the Altar, Christ lives in us; his body has passed into the substance of our bodies; his blood flows in our veins. For "he that eats my flesh and drinks my blood abides in me and I in him." These are his words. Christ grows in us, and we grow in him, until being thoroughly formed by him, we attain to the full stature of Jesus Christ, and everything we do or are, "whether we eat or sleep, or whatsoever we do," our work, our recreation, our pleasures and our pains, are all taken up into the Christ-life.

The consciousness of this mystery should pass in all its joyous strength and beauty into our very manner of walking. The command "to walk before the Lord and be perfect" is a profound figure of speech. We ought both to fulfil the command and illustrate the figure.

But in sober reality. Beauty of this order is not the product of mere wishing.

STRIKING THE BREAST

W<small>HEN</small> the priest begins Holy Mass, while he is standing at the foot of the altar, the faithful, or the servers in their stead, say "I confess to Almighty God . . . that I have sinned exceedingly in thought, word and deed, through my fault, through my fault, through my most grievous fault," and each time they confess their guilt they strike their breasts. What is the significance of this striking the breast?

All its meaning lies in its being rightly done. To brush one's clothes with the tips of one's fingers is not to strike the breast. We should beat upon our breasts with our closed fists. In the old picture of Saint Jerome in the desert he is kneeling on the ground and striking his breast with a stone. It is an honest blow, not an elegant gesture. To strike the breast is to beat against the gates of our inner world in order to shatter them. This is its significance.

That world, that inner world, should be full of light, strength, and active energy. Is it? We should engage most earnestly in the search to find out how it really stands with us within. What has our response been to the grave demands made on us by duty? By our neighbors' needs? By the decisions we were called on to make? Scarcely anything stirs in answer. We have loaded ourselves with innumerable offences. Do they trouble us? "In the midst of life we are in death." We hardly give it a thought. "Awake, look into yourself, bethink yourself, reflect, repent, do penance." It is the voice of God. Striking the breast is the visible sign that we hear that summons. Let the blow penetrate. Let it rouse up that sleeping inner world. Let it wake us up, and make us see, and turn to God.

And when we do reflect, what do we see? We see our lives trifled away, God's commandments transgressed, duties neglected, "through my fault, through my fault, through my most grievous fault." A world of guilt lies imprisoned within our breasts. There is but one way to get rid of it, by the whole-hearted confession that "I have sinned in thought, word and deed against God most holy, against the communion of saints." The soul moves over to the side of God and takes his part against herself. We think of ourselves as God thinks of us. We are stirred to anger against ourselves on account of our sins, and we punish ourselves with a blow.

The blow also is to wake us up. It is to shake the soul awake into the consciousness that God is calling, so that she may hear, and take his part and punish herself. She reflects, repents and is contrite. It is for this reason that priest and people strike their breasts when they confess their sins at the foot of the altar.

Before Communion also we strike our breasts when the priest holds up for us to see the Body of the Lord, and we say, "Lord, I am not worthy that thou shouldst enter under my roof, and again, in the litany when we confess our guilt and say, "We sinners beseech thee to hear us." But in these customs the force of the meaning of the rite has been weakened, as it has been also when the Host or Chalice is lifted up, or in the Angelus at the words, "The Word was made flesh and dwelt among us." The gesture in these instances has come to mean no more than reverence or humility. Its astringency should be restored. It is a summons to repentance and to the self-inflicted punishment of a contrite heart.

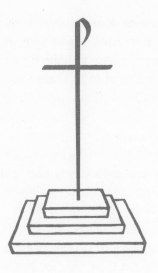

STEPS

THE more we think about these long-familiar things the clearer does their meaning grow. Things we have done thousands of times, if we will only look into them more deeply, will disclose to us their beauty. If we will listen, they will speak.

After their meaning has been revealed to us, the next step is to enter upon our inheritance and make what we have long possessed really our own. We must learn how to see, how to hear, how to do things the right way.

Such a learning-by-looking, growing-by-learning, is what matters. Regarded any other way these things keep their secret. They remain dark and mute. Regarded thus, they yield to us their essential nature, that nature which formed them to their outward shapes. Make trial for yourself. The most commonplace everyday objects and actions hide matters of deepest import. Under the simplest exteriors lie the greatest mysteries.

Steps are an instance. Every one of the innumerable times we go upstairs a change, though too slight and subtle to be perceptible, takes place in us. There is something mysterious in the act of ascending. Our intelligence would be puzzled to explain it, but instinctively we feel that it is so. We are made that way.

When the feet mount the steps, the whole man, including his spiritual substance, goes up with them. All ascension, all going up, if we will but give it thought, is motion in the direction of that high place where everything is great, everything made perfect.

For this sense we have that heaven is "up" rather than "down" we depend on something in us deeper than our reasoning powers. How can God be up or down? The only approach to God is by becoming better morally, and what has spiritual improvement to do with a material action like going up a pair of stairs? What has pure being to do with a rise in the position of our bodies? There is no explanation. Yet the natural figure of speech for what is morally bad is baseness, and a good and noble action we call a high action. In our minds we make a connection, unintelligible but real, between rising up and the spiritual approach to God; and Him we call the All-Highest.

So the steps that lead from the street to the church remind us that in going up into the house of prayer we are coming nearer to God; the steps from the nave to the choir, that we are entering in before the All-Holy. The steps between the choir and the altar say to whoever ascends them the same words that God spoke to Moses on Mount Horeb: "Put your shoes from off your feet, for the place whereon thou standest is holy ground." The altar is the threshold of eternity.

It is a great idea that if we go up even a common stairway with our minds on what we are doing, we really do leave below the base and trivial, and are in actual fact ascending up on high. Words are not very adequate; but the Christian knows that when he ascends it is the Lord that ascends. In him the Lord repeats his own ascension. That is what steps mean.

DOORS

EVERYTIME we enter a church, if we but notice it, a question is put to us. Why has a church doors? It seems a foolish question. Naturally, to go in by. Yes, but doors are not necessary — only a doorway. An opening with a board partition to close it off would be a cheap and practical convenience of letting people out and in. But the door serves more than a practical use; it is a re-minder.

When you step through the doorway of a church

you are leaving the outer-world behind and entering an inner world. The outside world is a fair place abounding in life and activity, but also a place with a mingling of the base and ugly. It is a sort of market place, crossed and recrossed by all and sundry. Perhaps "unholy" is not quite the word for it, yet there is something profane about the world. Behind the church doors is an inner place, separated from the market place, a silent, consecrated and holy spot. It is very certain that the whole world is the work of God and his gift to us, that we may meet Him anywhere, that everything we receive is from God's hand, and, when received religiously, is holy. Nevertheless men have always felt that certain precincts were in a special manner set apart and dedicated to God.

Between the outer and the inner world are the doors. They are the barriers between the market place and the sanctuary, between what belongs to the world at large and what has become consecrated to God. And the door warns the man who opens it to go inside that he must now leave behind the thoughts, wishes and cares which here are out of place, his curiosity, his vanity, his worldly interests, his secular self. "Make yourself clean. The ground you tread is holy ground."

Do not rush through the doors. Let us take time to open our hearts to their meaning and pause a moment beforehand so as to make our entering-in a fully intended and recollected act.

The doors have yet something else to say. Notice how as you cross the threshold you unconsciously lift your head and your eyes, and how as you survey the great interior space of the church there also takes place in you an inward expansion and enlargement. Its great width and height have an analogy to infinity and eternity. A church is a similitude of the heavenly dwelling place of God. Mountains indeed are higher, the wide blue sky outside stretches immeasurably further. But whereas outside space is unconfined and formless, the portion of space set aside for the church has been formed, fashioned, designed at every point with God in view. The long pillared aisles, the width and solidity of the walls, the high arched and vaulted roof, bring home to us that this is God's house and the seat of his hidden presence.

It is the doors that admit us to this mysterious place. Lay aside, they say, all that cramps and narrows, all that sinks the mind. Open your heart, lift up your eyes. Let your soul be free, for this is God's temple.

It is likewise the representation of you, yourself. For you, your soul and your body, are the living temple of God. Open up that temple, make it spacious, give it height.

Lift up your heads, O ye gates,

and be ye lifted up, ye everlasting doors,

and the King of Glory shall come in.

Heed the cry of the doors. Of small use to you is a house of wood and stone unless you yourself are God's living dwelling. The high arched gates may be lifted up, and the portals parted wide, but unless the doors of your heart are open, how can the King of Glory enter in?

CANDLES

WE stand in a double and contrary relationship to objects outside ourselves. We stand to the world and all its contents as when God brought the animals to the first man for him to name. Among them all Adam could find no companion. Between man and the rest of creation there is a barrier of difference, which neither scientific knowledge nor moral depravity can remove or efface. Man is of another make from every other earthly creature. To him they are foreign. His kinship is with God.

On the other hand he is related to everything that exists in the world. Everywhere we feel somehow at home. The shapes, attitudes, movements of objects all speak to us, all are a means of communication. It is the incessant occupation of the human soul to express through them its own interior life, and to make them serve as its signs and symbols. Every notable form we come across strikes us as expressing something in our own nature, and reminds us of ourselves.

This feeling of our connection with things is the source of metaphor and simile. We are profoundly estranged from, yet mysteriously connected with, outside objects. They are not us, and yet all that is or happens is an image to us of ourselves.

One of these image-objects strikes me, and I think most people, as having more than ordinary force and beauty. It is that of a lighted candle. There it rises, firmly fixed in the metal cup on the broad-based, long-shafted candlestick, spare and white, yet not wan, distinct against whatever background, consuming in the little flame that flickers above it the pure substance of the wax in softly-shining light. It seems a symbol of selfless generosity. It stands so unwavering in its place, so erect, so clear and disinterested, in perfect readiness to be of service. It stands, where it is well to stand, before God.

It stands in its appointed place, self-consumed in light and warmth.

Yes, of course the candle is unconscious of what it does. It has no soul. But we can give it a soul by making it an expression of our own attitude.

Stir up in yourself the same generous readiness to be used. "Lord, here am I." Let the clean, spare, serviceable candle bespeak your own attitude. Let your readiness grow into steadfast loyalty. Even as this candle, O Lord, would I stand in your presence.

Do not weaken in or try to evade your vocation. Persevere. Do not keep asking why and to what purpose. To be consumed in truth and love, in light and warmth, for God, is the profoundest purpose of human life.

HOLY WATER

WATER is a mysterious thing. It is so clear and friction-less, so "modest," as St. Francis called it. It hardly pretends to any character of its own. It seems to have no other end or object than to be of service, to cleanse what is soiled and to refresh what is dry.

But at some time you must have gazed down into the still depths of a great body of water, and felt it tugging to draw you in, and have got a glimpse of the strange and secret thing water is, and of the marvels, terrors and enticements that lurk in its depths. Or, at another time when it was whipped to a boiling torrent by a storm, you have heard it rushing and roaring, rushing and roaring, and watched the sucking vortex of a whirlpool and felt a force so grim and dreary that you had to tear your thoughts away.

It is indeed a strange element. On the one hand smooth and transparent, as if it hardly existed in its own right, ready at hand to wash away dirt and satisfy thirst; and on the other a restless, foundationless, enigmatic force that entices us on to destruction. It is a proper image for the secret ground-source from which life issues and back into which death recalls it. It is an apt image for this life of ours that looks so clear and is so inexplicable.

It is plain why the church uses water as the sign and the bearer of the divine life of grace. We emerge from the waters of baptism into a new life, born again of water and the Holy Ghost. In those same waters the old man was destroyed and put to death.

With this elemental element, that yields no answer to our questioning, with this transparent, frictionless, fecund fluid, this symbol and means of the supernatural life of grace, we make on ourselves, from forehead to breast, from shoulder to shoulder, the sign of the cross.

By her consecration of it, the Church has freed water from the dark powers that sleep in it. This is not a form of language. Anyone whose perceptions have not been blunted must be aware of the powers of natural magic inherent in water. And are they only natural powers? Is there not present also a dark and preternatural power? In nature, for all her richness and beauty, there is something demonic. City life has so deadened our senses that we have lost our perception of it. But the Church knows it is there. She "exorcises" out of water those divinities that are at enmity with God. She blesses it and asks God to make of it a vehicle of his grace. Therefore the Christian when he enters church moistens forehead, breast and shoulders, all his person, with the clean and cleansing water in order to make clean his soul. It is a pleasing custom that brings grace and nature freed from sin, and man, who so longs for cleanness, into the unity of the sign of the cross.

At evening also we sign ourselves in holy water. Night, as the proverb says, is no friend to man. Our human nature is formed and fashioned for light. Just before we give ourselves over into the power of sleep and darkness, and the light of day and consciousness is extinguished, there is a satisfaction in making the sign of the cross on ourselves with holy water. Holy water is the symbol of nature set free from sin. May God protect us from every form of darkness! And at morning, when we emerge again out of sleep, darkness and unconsciousness, and life begins afresh, we do the same thing. But in the morning it is to remind ourselves of that holy water from which we have issued into the light of Christ. The soul-redeemed and nature redeemed encounter one another in the sign of the cross.

FIRE

SOME cold, dull day in late autumn, when darkness is coming on, and the wide plain below as far as eye can reach is empty of life, and the mountain-path chill underfoot, and we are feeling very much alone, a strong natural desire comes over us for human contact. Then, suddenly, at a turn of the road, a light beams out. It comes like the answer to a summons, like a thing expectation called for, like a missing link in a series suddenly supplied.

Or, you are sitting at dusk in a dreary room between blank walls among uncongenial furniture. A familiar step approaches, a practiced hand sets the hearth to rights, the kindling crackles, a flame shoots up and the room glows with comfortable warmth. The change is as pleasant as when a cold inexpressive face suddenly lights up with friendliness.

Fire is closely allied to life. It is the aptest symbol we have for the soul within that makes us live. Like fire, life is warm and radiant, never still, eager for what is out of reach. When we watch the leaping tongues of flame, as they follow every current of the draught, soaring up not to be diverted, radiating waves of light and heat, we feel how exact the parallel is, how deep the kinship. This fire that forces its way through the intractable material that impedes it and reaches out to touch with light the things around and make for them a center of illumination, — what an image it is of that mysterious flame in us that has been set alight to penetrate the whole of nature and provide it with a hearth!

And if this aspiring, irresistible, life of ours were allowed to express itself outwardly, if it were given the least outlet, it also would break through and burst into flame.

And with what strength it should burn before the altar where at all times it rightfully belongs! We should stand there close to the Sacramental Presence where God addresses himself to us and we address ourselves to God, concentrating our force and our intelligence in prayer and attention. We recognize in the lamp before the altar the image and representation of what our life should be. Its flame is never allowed to go out.

As material light it has of course nothing to say to God. It is for you to make it an expression of your soul, like it burning out the force of your life in flame and light close to the Holy Presence.

We cannot learn this all at once. It must be striven for. But each moment of quiet illumination will bring you nearer to God, and will carry you back among men at peace. You leave the sanctuary lamp before the tabernacle in your stead, saying to God, "Lord, it stands for my soul, which is at all times in thy presence."

ASHES

On the edge of the woods grows a larkspur. Its glorious blue blossom rising on its bending stalk from among the dark green curiously-shaped leaves fills the air with color. A passerby picks the flower, loses interest in it and throws it into the fire, and in a short moment all that is left of that splendid show is a thin streak of grey ash.

What fire does in an instant, time is always doing to everything that lives. The delicate fern, the stout mullein, the rooted oak, butterflies, darting swallows, nimble squirrels, heavy oxen, all of them, equally, sooner or later, by accident, disease, hunger, cold, — all these clear-cut forms, all this flourishing life, turns to a little ash, a handful of dry dust, which every breeze scatters this way and that. All this brilliant color, all this sensitive, breathing life, falls into pale, feeble, dead earth, and less than earth, into ashes. It is the same with ourselves. We look into an opened grave and shiver: a few bones, a handful of ash-grey dust.

> Remember man
> that dust thou art
> and unto dost shalt thou return.

Ashes signify man's overthrow by time. Our own swift passage, ours and not someone else's, ours, mine. When at the beginning of Lent the priest takes the burnt residue of the green branches of the last Palm Sunday and inscribes with it on my forehead the sign of the cross, it is to remind me of my death.

> Memento homo
> quia pulvis est
> et in pulverem reverteris.

Everything turns to ashes, everything whatever. This house I live in, these clothes I am wearing, my household stuff, my money, my fields, meadows, woods, the dog that follows me, my horse in his stall, this hand I am writing with, these eyes that read what I write, all the rest of my body, people I have loved, people I have hated, or been afraid of, whatever was great in my eyes upon earth, whatever small and contemptible, all without exception will fall back into dust.

INCENSE

"AND I saw an angel come and stand before the altar, having a golden censer; and there was given to him much incense, and the smoke of the incense of the prayers of the saints ascended up before God from the hand of the angel." So writes Saint John in the mysterious book of the Apocalypse.

The offering of an incense is a generous and beautiful rite. The bright grains of incense are laid upon the red-hot charcoal, the censer is swung, and the fragrant smoke rises in clouds. In the rhythm and the sweetness there is a musical quality; and like music also is the entire lack of practical utility: it is a prodigal waste of precious material. It is a pouring out of unwithholding love.

"When the Lord was at supper Mary brought the spikenard of great price and poured it over his feet and wiped them with her hair, and the house was filled with the odor of the ointment." Narrower spirits objected. "Whereto this waste?" But the Son of God has spoken, "Let her alone. She hath done it against my burial." Mary's anointing was a mystery of death and love and the sweet savour of sacrifice.

The offering of incense is like Mary's anointing at Bethany. It is as free and objectless as beauty. It burns and is consumed like love that lasts through death. And the arid soul still takes his stand and asks the same question: What is the good of it?

It is the offering of a sweet savour which Scripture itself tells us is the prayers of the Saints. Incense is the symbol of prayer. Like pure prayer it has in view no object of its own; it asks nothing for itself. It rises like the Gloria at the end of a psalm in adoration and thanksgiving to God for his great glory.

It is true that symbolism of this sort may lead to mere aestheticism. There are imaginations in which the fragrant clouds of incense induce a spurious religiosity; and, in such instances, when it does so, the Christian conscience does right to protest that prayer should be made in spirit and in truth. But though prayer is a plain, straight-forward business, it is not the so-much-for-so-muchness which the niggardly imagination and flesh-less heart of the religious Philistine would make of it. The same spirit persists that produced the objection of Judas of Kerioth. Prayer is not to be measured by its bargaining power; it is not a matter of bourgeois common sense.

Minds of this order know nothing of that magnanimous prayer that seeks only to give. Prayer is a profound act of worship, that asks neither why nor wherefore. It rises like beauty, like sweetness, like love. The more there is in it of love, the more of sacrifice. And when the fire has wholly consumed the sacrifice, a sweet savour ascends.

LIGHT AND HEAT

THE heart's deepest need makes us long for union with God. Two paths lead to this union, two separate paths, though they end at the same goal. The first is the path of knowledge and love. This path our own souls point out to us. The other we know only because Christ has shown it to us.

The act of knowing is an act of union. By knowledge we penetrate the nature of an object and make the object our own. We mentally absorb it, and it becomes part and parcel of ourselves. Love is also an act of union, of union, and not merely of the desire of union. It is an actual union, for so much of a thing as we love that much belongs to us. Since there are more ways than one of loving, we call this kind "spiritual" love. But the word is not quite right, since it also applies to the other mode of union by the second path I spoke of. The difference is that while this first instinctive kind of love effects a union, it does not, as the other does, join being with being. It is union by conscious knowledge and willed intention.

Does any material form exist that provides a likeness for such a union? There does; the very wonderful one of light and heat.

Our eyes, without approaching or touching it, see and take in the candle flame. Eyes and candle remain where they were, and yet a union is effected. It is not a union of mingling and absorption, but the chaste and reverent union of the soul with God by knowledge. Since, as Scripture says, God is truth, and since whoever knows the truth, mentally possesses it, so by right knowledge of him our minds possess God. God is present in the intellect whose thoughts of him are true. This is what is meant by "knowing God". To know God is to be one with him as the eye becomes one with the candle flame by looking at it.

But the light of the candle flame cannot be separated from its heat. Though again the candle remains where it was, we feel on our cheek or the back of our hand a radiating warmth.

This union of heat is a likeness for the union between us and the Divine Flame by love. God is good. Whoever loves the good possesses it spiritually, for the good becomes ours by our loving it. Just so much of goodness as we love, just that much do we possess. "God," as Saint John tells us, "is love. And he that abideth in love abideth in God, and God in him." To know, to love God, is to be one with him; and our eternal beatitude will consist in looking upon God and loving him. Looking, loving, does not mean that we stand hungering in his presence, but that to our innermost depths we are filled and satisfied.

Flame, which is a figure for the soul, is also a figure for the living God; for "God is light and in him there is no darkness." As the flame radiates light so God radiates truth, and the soul by receiving truth is united with God, as our eyes by seeing its light are united with the flame. And, as the flame radiates heat, so does God radiate the warmth of goodness; and as the hand and the cheek by perceiving the warmth become one with the flame, so whoever loves God becomes one with him in goodness. But also, just as the candle remains free and disengaged in its place, so does God abide unmoved "dwelling in unapproachable light."

Flame, emitting light, emitting heat, is an image to us of the living God.

All this comes very much home to us on Holy Saturday when the Easter candle, which symbolizes Christ; is lighted. Three times, each time in a higher tone, the deacon sings "Lumen Christi," and then lights the Pascal candle. At once every lamp and candle in the church is lighted from it, and the whole building is alight and aglow with the radiance and warmth of God's presence.

BREAD AND WINE

But there is another path that leads to God. Had not Christ's own words made it known to us so plainly, and the liturgy repeated them with so assured a confidence, we should not be bold enough to speak of it. Seeing God, loving God, by consciously turning toward him with our minds and wills, though a real union, is yet not a union of being with being. It is not only our minds and our wills that strive to possess God. As the psalm says, "My heart and my flesh are athirst for the living God." Only then shall we be at rest when our whole being is joined to his. Not by any mingling or confusion of natures, for creature and creator are forever distinct, and to suppose otherwise would be as nonsensical as it is presumptuous. Nevertheless, besides the union of simple love and knowledge, there is another union, that of life and being.

We desire, are compelled to desire, this union, and the Scripture and the Liturgy place upon our lips words that give profound expression to our longing. As the body desires food and drink, just so closely does our individual life desire to be united with God. We hunger and thirst after God. It is not enough for us to know him and to love him. We would clasp him, draw him to ourselves, hold him fast, and, bold as it sounds, we would take him into ourselves as we do our necessary food and drink, and thereby still and satisfy our hunger to the full.

The liturgy of Corpus Christi repeats to use these words of Christ: "As the living Father hath sent me, and I live by the Father, so he that eateth me, the same shall also live by me." Those are the words. For us to prefer such a claim as a thing due to us of right would border on blasphemy. But since it is God that speaks, we inwardly assent and believe.

But let us not presume on them as if in any way they effaced the boundary between creature and Creator.

In deepest reverence, and yet without fear, let us acknowledge the longing which God himself has planted in us, and rejoice in this gift of his exceeding goodness. "My flesh," Christ says to us, "is food indeed, and my blood is drink indeed . . . He that eateth my flesh and drinketh my blood abideth in me and I in him . . . As the Father hath given me to have life in myself, so he that eateth me, the same also shall live by me." To eat his flesh, to drink his blood, to eat him, to absorb into ourselves the living God — it is beyond any wish me might be capable of forming for ourselves, yet it satisfies to the full what we long for, — of necessity long for, — from the bottom of our souls.

Bread is food. It is wholesome, nourishing food for which we never lose our appetite. Under the form of bread God becomes for us even the food of life. "We break a bread," writes Saint Ignatius of Antioch to the faithful at Ephesus, "we break a bread that is the food of immortality." By this food our being is so nourished with God himself that we exist in him and he in us.

Wine is drink. To be exact, it is more than drink, more than a liquid like water that merely quenches thirst. "Wine that maketh glad the heart of man" is the biblical expression. The purpose of wine is not only to quench thirst, but also to give pleasure and satisfaction and exhilaration. "My cup, how goodly it is, how plenteous!" Literally, how intoxicating, though not in the sense of drinking to excess. Wine possesses a sparkle, a perfume, a vigour, that expands and clears the imagination. Under the form of wine Christ gives us his divine blood. It is no plain and sober draught. It was bought at a great price, at a divinely excessive price. Sanguis Christi, inebria me, prays Saint Ignatius, that Knight of the Burning Heart. In one of the antiphons for the feast of Saint Agnes, the blood of Christ is called a mystery of ineffable beauty. "I have drawn milk and honey from his lips, and his blood hath given fair color to my cheeks."

For our sakes Christ became bread and wine, food and drink. We make bold to eat him and to drink him. This bread gives us solid and substantial strength. This wine bestows courage, joy out of all earthly measure, sweetness, beauty, limitless enlargement and perception. It brings life in intoxicating excess, both to possess and to impart.

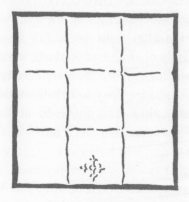

LINEN

THE altar is covered with a linen cloth. The corporal, which, as representing the winding-sheet of Christ's body, is laid under Host and Chalice, is made of linen. The priest's alb, which is always worn during divine service, is of white linen. When the Holy Bread is being distributed a linen cloth covers the Lord's table.

Good linen, strong-fibered and close-woven, is a costly material. It has the lustre of fresh snow. Once when I came upon a patch of new-fallen snow lying among dark spruce trees, I turned aside and took my heavy boots another way, out of sheer respect. It is a sign of respect that we cover holy things with linen.

When the Holy Sacrifice is offered, the uppermost covering of the altar must be of fair linen. The high altar, in the Holy of Holies, represents, we said, the altar in man's soul. But it more than represents it. The two altars are inseparable. They are really, though mysteriously, the same altar. The authentic and perfect altar in which Christ's sacrifice is offered is the union of them both.

It is for this reason that linen makes its strong appeal. We have a sense that it corresponds to something within ourselves. It seems to make some claim upon us in the nature of a wish or a reproach. Only from a clean heart comes a right sacrifice. In the same measure as the heart is pure is the sacrifice pleasing to God.

Linen has much to teach us about the nature of purity. Genuine linen is an exquisite material. Purity is not the product of rude force or found in company with harsh manners. Its strength comes of its fineness. Its orderliness is gentle. But linen is also extremely strong; it is no gossamer web to flutter in every breeze. In real purity there is nothing of that sickly quality that flies from life and wraps itself up in unreal dreams and ideals out of its reach. It has the red cheeks of the man who is glad to be alive and the firm grip of the hard fighter.

And if we look a little further, it has still one thing more to say. It was not always so clean and fine as it now is. It was to begin with, unsightly stuff. In order to attain its present fragrant freshness it had to be washed and rewashed, and then bleached. Purity is not come by at the first. It is indeed a grace, and there are people who have so carried the gift in their souls that their whole nature has the strength and freshness of unsullied purity. But they are the exception. What is commonly called purity is no more than the doubtful good of not having been shaken by the storms of life. Purity, that is really such, is attained not at the beginning but at the end of life, and achieved only by long and courageous effort.

So the linen on the altar in its fine white durableness stands to us both for exquisite cleanness of heart and for fibrous strength.

There is a place in Saint John's Apocalypse where mention is made of "a great multitude which no man could number, of all nations and tribes and peoples and tongues, standing before the throne clothed in white robes." And a voice asked, "Who are these and whence come they?" And the answer is given: "These are they who are come out of great tribulation, and have washed their robes and made them white in the blood of the

Lamb. Therefore they are before the throne of God, and they serve him day and night.""Let me be clothed, O Lord, in a white garment," is the priest's prayer while he is putting on the alb for the Holy Sacrifice.

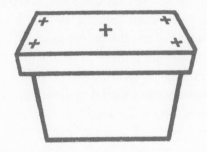

THE ALTAR

MANY and various are the forces that actuate a human being. Man has the power to embrace the whole world of nature, its stars, mountains, seas and great rivers, its trees and animals, and the human world in which he finds himself, and by love and appreciation to draw it all into his own inner world. He has the power of love, the power also of hate and repulsion. He can oppose and repudiate his surroundings or refashion them after his own mind. Impulses of pleasure, desire, trust, love, calm-

73

ness, excitement course through his heart in multitudinous waves.

But of all his powers man possesses none nobler than his ability to recognize that there is a being higher than his own, and to bind himself to the honor of this Higher Being. Man has the power to know God, to worship him, and devote himself to him in order "that God may be glorified."

But if the majesty of God is to illuminate him wholly, if he is so to adore the Divine Majesty as to free himself from his persistent self-seeking, — if he is to slip out of himself and go beyond himself and so attain to a worship of God that is for God's glory only, — then he must exert a still higher power.

In the still depths of man's being there is a region of calm light, and there he exercises the soul's deepest power, and sends up sacrifice to God.

The external representation of this region of central calm and strength is the altar.

The altar occupies the holiest spot in the church. The church has itself been set apart from the world of human work, and the altar is elevated above the rest of the church in a spot as remote and separate as the sanctuary of the soul. The solid base it is set on is like the human will that knows that God has instituted man for his worship and is determined to perform that wor-

74

ship faithfully. The table of the altar that rests upon this base stands open and accessible for the presentation of sacrifice. It is not in a dark recess where the actions may be dimly glimpsed, but uncurtained, unscreened, a level surface in plain sight, placed, as the heart's altar should be placed, open in the sight of God without proviso or reservation.

The two altars, the one without and the one within, belong inseparably together. The visible altar at the heart of the church is but the external representation of the altar at the centre of the human breast, which is God's temple, of which the church with its walls and arches is but the expression and figure.

THE CHALICE

YEARS ago, and only once, I came upon a chalice. *The* chalice. I had of course seen many chalices, but this one was not only seeing; it was a meeting, an encounter. It was at Beuron when a kindly monk in charge of the sacred vessels was showing me the treasures of the sacristy.

The broad base it stood on adhered firmly to the ground. The stem, sharp, spare and delicately thin, seemed to lift itself with compressed force and carrying power. A little more than half way up it expanded in a knob, and then at the top, first confining its strength in a narrow ring or band in orderly compression, it broke out into a wealth of foliation, finely cut but strong, in which lay the cup, the heart of the chalice.

From this chalice I caught a glimpse of the meaning of the sacrament. The sure-footed base, the long shaft molded to carry weight, the disciplined, ingathered strength blossoming out into a cup, open but enclosed, could signify but one thing: to receive and retain.

The pure and holy vessel of the mystery receives and guards in its dimly shining depths the divine drops of the gracious, fruitful blood, which is sheer fire, sheer love.

I had a further thought, an insight or rather, an intuition. The chalice represents the created universe. That universe has but one purpose and one final meaning: man, the living creature, with his soul and body and his restless heart . . . Saint Augustine has a great saying: "That which makes a man to be what he is is his capacity to receive God and hold him fast."

THE PATEN

ONE morning I had climbed a high hill and was turning around to go back. Below me, in the early light, ringed around with the silent hills, lay the lake, crystal clear. Great green trees bordered it with their nobly-sweeping boughs. The sky was high and spacious. The whole scene was so fresh, so clear, that a feeling of joy took possession of me. It was as if invisible noiseless fountains were shooting up into the bright, far, distance.

Then I came to understand how a man, whose heart is overflowing, may stand with uplifted face, and hands outspread like the shallow dish of the paten, and offer up to the Infinite Goodness, to the Father of lights, to God, who is love, the world around him and within him, the silent world brimming over with life and light, and how it would seem to him that that world, lifted up on the paten of his open hands, would be clean and holy.

Thus did Christ once stand on the spiritual mount and offer up to his Father the holocaust of his love and his life's breath. On a lower eminence of that same mountain, on the foothill of Mount Moriah, Abraham performed his sacrifice. And in the same spot before this the King and Priest Melchisidech had made expiation. In the self-same place, in the first age of the world, Abel's simple offering rose straight up to heaven.

That spiritual mountain still rises, and the hand of God is still stretched out above, and the gift mounts up every time a priest — not in his own person, since he is merely the instrument, of no value in itself, — stands at the altar and raises in his outspread hands the paten with the white bread on it. "Receive, O Holy Father, almighty, everlasting God, this spotless victim, which I, thine unworthy servant, offer to thee, O God, living and true, for all my countless sins and negligences, and for all those here present . . . that it may avail for my and their salvation into life everlasting."

BLESSING

HE alone can bless that has the power. He alone is able to bless who is able to create. God alone can bless.

God, when he blesses his creature, looks upon him and calls him by his name and brings his all powerful love to bear upon the pith and centre of his being and pours out from his hand the power of fruitfulness, the power of growth and increase, of health and goodness. "I will keep mine eye upon you and make you to increase."

Only God can bless. Blessing is the disposition to be made of what a thing is or effects. It is the word of power of the Master of Creation. It is the promise and assurance of the Lord of Providence. Blessing bestows a happy destiny.

Nietzsche's remark, that instead of asking favours we should confer blessings, is the saying of a rebel. He well understood his own meaning. God only can bless since God only is the master of life. By our nature we are petitioners. The contrary of blessing is cursing. A curse is a sentence and a seal of mischief. It is, like blessing, a judgment imprinted upon the forehead and the heart. It shuts off the sources of life.

God has imparted a portion of his power to bless and to curse to those whose vocation it is to create life. Parents possess this power: "The blessing of the father establisheth the houses of the children." Priests possess it. As parents engender natural life, so the priest begets the supernatural life of grace. To give life is the nature and office of both.

And he also may attain to the power of blessing who no longer seeks himself but in perfect simplicity of heart wills to be the servant of him Who has life in himself.

But the power to bless is always and only from God. It fails wholly if we assume it of ourselves. By nature we are petitioners, blessers only by God's grace, — just as we have the virtue of authority, of effectual command, only by God's grace.

What applies to blessing applies also to cursing. "The mother's curse rooteth up the foundations of the children's houses," that is to say of their life and their well-being.

All the forms of nature are prefigurements of grace. The power of effectual blessing, the power which the blessing actually conveys, the real, the essential power, of which our natural life is but a figure, is God's own life. It is with himself that God blesses. The divine life is begotten by God's blessing. By it we are made sharers in the divine nature by a pure gift, a grace, bestowed on us by Christ. So also the sign of the cross is a blessing in which God bestows upon us himself.

This power of divine blessings is merely lent to those who stand in God's stead. Fathers and mothers have it by the sacrament of Christian marriage. The priest has it by the sacrament of ordination. By virtue of the sacrament of baptism and the sacrament of confirmation, — which makes us kings and priests to God, — there is given to those "who love God with all their heart and all their mind and all their strength and their neighbors as themselves" the power to bless with God's own life. To each of these the power of blessing is given with such difference as the nature of his apostleship determines.

The visible representation of blessing is the hand. By its position and action it indicates the purpose of the blessing. In Confirmation it is laid on the head so that the Spirit which has its source in God may flow through it. When the hand signs the cross on forehead or breast it is in order that the divine plenitude may be poured out unstintedly. The hand, as it is the instrument of making and shaping, is also the instrument of spending and giving.

Finally there is the blessing given not by the hand but by the All Holy himself with the sacramental body of Christ. Let it be bestowed in profound reverence and subjection to the mystery.

SPACE SANCTIFIED

OF natural space we commonly predicate three directions, — up, down, and beside. They indicate that in space there is order, and that it is not a chaos. They enable us to conduct a mode of life and move about from place to place, erect buildings and live in them.

In divine and supernatural space there is also this order of direction. It is grounded in a mystery.

Churches are built along the east to west direction of the sun's course. They face the east and the rising sun. The chord of the sun's arc runs through them. They are built to receive his first and his last rays. The sun of the supernatural world is Christ. Consequently the course of the natural sun, his symbol, governs all sacred architecture and determines all its forms and arrangements. At every line and point eternal life is kept in view.

At the reading of the Gospel the missal is moved over to the left, that is, since the altar always faces east, it is moved toward the north. As a matter of history the divine message proceeded northward from the Mediterranean region, and the memory of this fact is present. But the more profound symbolism is that the south is the region of light, and signifies the divine illumination, as the north signifies darkness and cold. The Word of God, who is the Light of the World, rises out of the light and shines upon the darkness and presses hard upon it in order to make itself "comprehended."

East to west, south to north. The third direction is from above down, from below up. When he is preparing the Holy Sacrifice, the priest lifts up first the paten, then the chalice. God is above; he is the All-Highest. "Out of the depths" the suppliant lifts up hands and eyes toward the holy hills. The bishop, when he gives his blessing, lowers his hand upon the head of the person kneeling before him; the priest, when he consecrates, upon the objects to be blessed. Creation is a downward act, blessing comes down from above, from the Holy One on High. This third direction of supernatural space is proper to the soul and to God. Desire, prayer, sacrifice ascend upward from below; grace, the granting of prayer, the sacraments, descend downward from above.

In accordance with these directions the worshipper faces the rising sun, and turns his gaze upon Christ, whom it symbolizes. The divine light streams westward into the believer's heart. West to east is the soul's orientation; east to west the rise and progress of God.

From the north the darkness looks toward the light of the divine word; and from the fiery heart of the south the divine word streams out upon the darkness in light and warmth.

From beneath upward, out of the depths toward the throne of God on high, the soul sends up her yearnings, prayers and sacrifices; and God's response in grace, blessing, sacrament, comes downward from above.

BELLS

SPACE enclosed within the walls of a church reminds us of God. It has been made over to him as his own possession and is filled with his presence. Walled round, vaulted over, shut off from the world, it is turned inward toward the God who hides himself in mystery.

But what of space unenclosed, that vast expanse that stretches over the level earth on all sides, boundless, high above the highest hills, filling the deepest valleys which those hills encircle? Has it no connection with things holy?

It has indeed, and the symbol of this connection is the steeple with its bells.

The steeple is an integral part of God's house, and rises out of it up into the free air, and takes possession of all wide space in God's name. And the heavy bronze bells in the belfrey tower, so beautifully molded, swing about their shaft and send out peal on peal in waves of good loud sound. High and quick, or full-toned and measured, or roaring deep and slow, they pour out a flood of sound that fills the air with news of the Kingdom.

News from afar, news of the infinitely limitless God, news of man's bottomless desire, and of its inexhaustible fulfilment.

The bells are a summons to those "men of desire" whose hearts are open to far-off things.

The sound of bells stirs in us the feeling of distance. When they clang out from a steeple rising above a wide plain and their sound is carried to every point of the compass, and on and on to the hazy blue horizon, our wishes follow them as long as they are audible, until it comes home to us that there is no satisfaction of desire in far distant hopes, or indeed in anything outside ourselves.

Or, when the pealing bells of a mountain-built

church flood the valley with their clamor or send the sound straight up to the zenith, the listener, straining to follow, feels his heart expand beyond its usual narrow limits.

Or again, the bell tones in some green glimmering forest may reach us faintly, as from a great distance, too far off to tell from where, and old memories stir, and we strive to catch the sounds and to remember what it is they remind us of.

At such moments we have a perception of the meaning of space. We feel the pull of height, and stretch our wings and try to respond to infinitude.

The bells remind us of the world's immensity and man's still more immeasurable desires, and that only in the infinite God we can find our peace.

O Lord, this my soul is wider than the world, its longing from depths deeper than any valley, the pain of desire is more troubling than the faint lost bell notes. Only thyself canst fill so vast an emptiness.

TIME SANCTIFIED

THOUGH each hour of the day has its own character, three hours stand out from the rest — morning, evening, and, half way between them, noonday, and have an aspect distinctively their own. These three hours the church has consecrated.

Of them all the morning hour wears the most shining face. It possesses the energy and brightness of a beginning. Mysteriously, each morning we are born again. We emerge out of sleep refreshed, renewed, with an invigorating sense of being alive. This newly infused feeling of our existence turns to a prayer of thanksgiving for life to him who gave it. With an impulse to action born of fresh energy we think of the day ahead and of the work to be done in it, and this impulse also becomes a prayer. We begin the day in God's name and strength and ask him to make our work a work for him.

This morning hour when life reawakens and we are more keenly aware of our existince, when we begin the day with gratitude for our creation and turn to our work with fresh creative power, is a holy hour.

It is plain how much depends on this first hour. It is the day's beginning. The day may be started without a beginning. The day may be slipped into without thought or intention. But such a day, without purpose or character, hardly deserves the name. It is no more than a torn-off scrap of time. A day is a journey. One must decide which way one is going. It is also a work, and as such requires to be willed. A single day is the whole of life. The whole of life is like a day. Each day should have its own distinct character.

The morning hour exercises the will, directs the intention, and sets our gaze wholly upon God.

Evening also has its mystery. The mystery of evening is death. The day draws to a close and we make ready to enter the silence of sleep. The vigour which came with the morning has by evening run down, and what we seek then is rest. The secret note of death is sounded; and though our imaginations may be too crowded with the day's doings or too intent on tomorrow's plans for us to hear it distinctly, some perception of it, however remote, does reach us. And there are evenings when we have very much the feeling that life is drawing on to the long night "wherein no man can work."

What matters is to have a right understanding of what death means. Dying is more than the end of life. Death is the last summons that life serves on us. Dying is the final, the all-decisive act. With individuals as with nations the events that precede extinction in themselves conclude and settle nothing. After the thing has happened, it remains to be determined, by nations as by individuals, what is to be made of it, how it is to be regarded. The past event is neither good nor evil; in itself it is nothing. It is the face we put upon it, our way of viewing it, that makes it what it is. A great calamity, let us say, has overtaken a nation. The event has happened, but it is not over with. The nation may give way to despair. It may also think the matter through again, rejudge it; and make a fresh start. Not until we have decided how to take it is the event, long past though it may be, completed. The deep significance of death is that it is the final sentence a man passes on his whole life. It is the definite character he stamps upon it. When he comes to die a man must decide whether he will or will not once more take his whole life in hand, be sorry for all he has done amiss, and plunge and recast it in the burning heat of repentence, give God humble thanks for what was well done, (to him be the honor!) and cast the whole upon God in entire abandonment. Or he may give way to despondency and weakly and ignobly let life slip from him. In this case life comes to no conclusion; it merely, without shape or character, ceases to be.

The high "art of dying" is to accept the life that is leaving us, and by a single act of affirmation put it into God's hands.

Each evening we should practice this high art of giving life an effectual conclusion by reshaping the past and impressing it with a final validity and an eternal character. The evening hour is the hour of completion. We stand then before God with a premonition of the day on which we shall stand before him face to face and give in our final reckoning. We have a sense of the past being past, with its good and evil, its losses and waste. We place ourselves before God to whom all time, past or future, is the living present, before God who is able to restore to the penitent even what is lost. We think back over the day gone by. What was not well done contrition seizes upon and thinks anew. For what was well done we give God humble thanks, sincerely taking no credit to ourselves. What we are uncertain about, or failed to accomplish, the whole sorry remnant, we sink in entire abandonment into God's all powerful love.

MIDDAY

In the morning we have a lively and agreeable sense that life is starting and is on the increase; then obstacles arise and we are slowed up. By noon for a short while we seem to stand quite still. A little later our sense of life declines; we grow weary, recover a little, and then subside into the quiescence of night.

Half way between the rising and the setting sun, when the day is at its height, comes a breathing space, a brief and wonderful moment. The future is not pressing and we do not look ahead; the day is not yet declining and we do not look back. It is a pause, but not of weariness; our strength and energy are still at the full.

For noonday is the pure present. It looks beyond itself, but not into space or time. It looks upon eternity.

Noon is a profound moment. In the stir and extroversion of a city it passes unperceived. But in the country, among cornfields and quiet pastures, when the horizon is glowing with heat, we perceive what a deep moment it is. We stand still and time falls away. Eternity confronts us. Every hour reminds us of eternity; but noon is its close neighbor. Time waits and holds its peace. The day is at the full and time is the pure present.

The day being at its height and eternity close by, let us attend to it and give it entrance. In the distance the Angelus, breaking the noontide silence, reminds us of our redemption. "In the beginning was the Word and the Word was with God . . . The angel of the Lord brought the message to Mary, and she conceived of the Holy Ghost. Behold the handmaid of the Lord, be it done unto me according to thy will . . . And the Word became flesh and dwelt among us."

At the noon hour of man's day, in the fulness of time, a member of the human race, on whom this fulness had come, stood and waited. Mary did not hurry to meet it. She looked neither before or after. The fulness of time, the simple present, the moment that gives entrance to eternity, was upon her. She waited. Eternity leaned over; the angel spoke, and the Eternal Word took flesh in her pure bosom.

Now in our day the Angelus proclaims the mystery. Each noonday, for each Christian soul, the noonday of mankind is again present. At every moment of time the fulness of time is audible. At all times our life is close neighbor to eternity. We should always hold ourselves in that quietude that attends upon and is open to eternity. But since the noise of living is so loud, let us pause at least at noon, at the hour the church has sanctified, and set aside the business we are engaged in, and stand in silence and listen to the angel of the Lord proclaiming that "while the earth lay in deepest silence the Eternal Lord leapt down from his royal throne" — then into the course of history for that once only, but since then at every moment into the human soul.

THE NAME OF GOD

HUMAN perception has been dulled. We have lost our awareness of some deep and subtle things. Among them the zest for words. Words have for us now only a surface existence. They have lost their power to shock and startle. They have been reduced to a fleeting image, to a thin tinkle of sound.

Actually a word is the subtle body of a spirit. Two things meet and find expression in a word: the substance of the object that makes the impact, and that portion of our spirit that responds to that particular object. At least these two ought to go to the making of words, and did when the first man made them.

In one of the early chapters of the Bible we are told that "God brought the animals to Adam to see what he would call them . ." Man, who has an ability to see and a mind open to impressions, looked through the outward form into the inner essence and spoke the name. The name was the response made by the human soul to the soul of the creature. Something in man, that particular part of himself that corresponded to the nature of that particular creature, stirred in answer, since man is the epitome and point of union of creation. These two things, (or rather this double thing) the nature of things outside and man's interior correspondence with them, being brought into lively contact, found utterance in the name.

In a name a particle of the universe is locked with a particle of human consciousness. So when the man spoke the name, the image of the actual object appeared in his mind together with the sound he had made in response to it. The name was the secret sign which opened to him the world without and the world within himself.

Words are names. Speech is the noble art of giving things the names that fit them. The thing as it is in its nature and the soul as it is in its nature were divinely intended to sound in unison.

But this inward connection between man and the rest of creation was interrupted. Man sinned, and the bond was torn apart. Things became alien, even hostile, to him. His eyes lost the clearness of their vision. He looked at nature with greed, with the desire to master her and with the shifty glance of the guilty. Things shut their real natures from him. He asserted himself so successfully that his own nature eluded him. When he lost his child-like vision, his soul fell away from him, and with it his wisdom and his strength.

With the loss of the true name, was broken that vital union between the two parts of creation, the human and the non-human, which in God's intention were to be indissolubly joined in the bonds of peace. Only some fragmentary image, some obscure, confused echo, still reaches us; and if on occasion we do hear a word that is really a name, we stop short and try but cannot quite catch its import, and are left puzzled and troubled with the painful sensation that paradise is lost.

But in our day even the sense that paradise is lost is lost. We are too superficial to be distressed by the loss of meaning, though we are more and more glib about the surface sense. We pass words from mouth to mouth as we do money from hand to hand and with no more attention to what they were meant to convey than to the inscription on the coins. The value-mark is all we notice. They signify something, but reveal nothing. So far from promoting the intercourse between man and nature they clatter out of us like coins from a cash register and with much the same consciousness as the machine has of their value.

Once in a great while we are shocked into attention. A word, perhaps in a book, may strike us with all its original force. The black and white signs grow luminous. We hear the voice of the thing named. There is the same astonished impact, the same intellectual insight, as in the primitive encounter. We are carried out of ourselves into the far depths of time when God summoned man to his first work of word-making. But too soon we are back where we were and the cash register goes clicking on.

It may have been the name of God that we thus met face to face. Remembering how words came to be, it is plain enough to us why the faithful under the Old Law never uttered the word, and substituted for it the word Lord. What made the Jews the peculiar and elect nation is that they with more immediacy than any other people perceived the reality and nearness of God, and had a stronger sense of his greatness, his transcendence and his fecundity. His name had been revealed to them by

Moses. He that is, that is my name. He that is being in itself, needing nothing, self-subsistent, the essence of being and of power.

To the Jews the name of God was the image of his being. God's nature shone in his name. They trembled before it as they had trembled before the Lord himself in Sinai. God speaks of his name as of himself. When he says of the Temple, "My name shall be there," he means by his name, himself. In the mysterious book of the Apocalyse he promises that those that come through tribulation shall be as pillars in the temple of God, and that he will write his name upon them; that is, that he will sanctify them and give them himself.

This is the sense in which we are to understand the commandment, Thou shalt not take the Name of the Lord thy God in vain. This is how we are to understand the word in the prayer our Savior taught us, "Hallowed be thy name," and in the precept to begin whatever we undertake in God's name.

God's name is full of hidden power. It shadows forth the nature of infinitude, and nature of him who is measureless plenitude and limitless sublimity.

In that name is present also what is deepest in man. There is a correspondence between God and man's inmost being, for to God man inseparably belongs. Created by God, for God, man is restless until he is wholly one with God. Our personalities have no other meaning or purpose than union with God in mutual love. Whatever of nobility man possessess, his soul's soul, is contained in the word God. He is my God, my source, my goal, the beginning and the end of my being, him I worship, him I long for, him to whom with sorrow I confess my sins.

Strictly, all that exists is the name of God. Let us therefore beseech him not to let us take it in vain, but to hallow it. Let us ask him to make his name our light in glory. Let us not bandy it about meaninglessly. It is beyond price, thrice holy.

Let us honor God's name as we honor God himself. In reverencing God's name we reverence also the holiness of our own souls.